YOU ARE FRIENDLY

WRITTEN BY TODD SNOW
ILLUSTRATED BY MELODEE STRONG

Maren Green Publishing, Inc.
Oak Park Heights, Minnesota

FOR STEPHANIE,
BECAUSE YOU ARE.
-T.S.

TO "THE CREW"
FOR ALWAYS BEING THE GREATEST
GROUP OF FRIENDS!
LOVE YA, MELODEE

Ages 4 and up

Maren Green Publishing, Inc.
5525 Memorial Avenue North, Suite 6
Oak Park Heights, MN 55082
Toll-free 800-287-1512

Text copyright © 2008 Todd Snow
Illustrations copyright © 2008 Melodee Strong

Library of Congress Cataloging-in-Publication Data is available.

Edited by Pamela Espeland

Text set in Garamond Pro and Wonderlism
Illustrations created using acrylic on wood

First Edition November 2008
10 9 8 7 6 5 4 3 2 1
Manufactured in China

ISBN 978-1-934277-18-8 (pbk.)

www.marengreen.com

YOU ARE FRIENDLY
IN MANY WAYS.

WHEN YOU HOLD AN ANIMAL GENTLY

AND PET IT SOFTLY.

WITH ANOTHER PERSON.

AND YOU GIVE
THE PERSON A HUG.

YOU ARE FRIENDLY WHEN YOU
MAKE ROOM FOR OTHERS

UNDER YOUR
UMBRELLA.

"CAN I HELP?"

YOU ARE FRIENDLY
WHEN YOU SAY "PLEASE"

AND "THANK YOU."

TO JOIN IN.

AND SAY
"SEE YOU LATER!"

Also available from Maren Green Publishing

ISBN 978-1-934277-19-5

You Are Brave *By Todd Snow, illustrated by Melodee Strong.* What does it mean to be brave? For children, it can mean meeting new people, trying new foods, and letting friends play with their toys. Each child is brave in his or her own ways. Written in simple words, vividly illustrated with realistic scenes that relate to children's everyday lives, *You Are Brave* lets young children know that bravery is about many things: feelings, actions, and being open to new experiences. *Paperback, full color, 8" x 8", 24 pages. Ages 4 & up.* MG119 **$8.99**
Also available in board book format: Full color, 6" x 6", 24 pages, Ages Baby—Preschool. (ISBN 978-1-934277-08-9) MG110 **$6.99**

You Are Healthy *By Todd Snow, illustrated by Melodee Strong.* Experts have identified key behaviors important to children's health. These include active play, eating right, washing hands, drinking water, getting enough sleep, and spending time with loved ones. This warm, inviting book introduces young children to things they can do to stay healthy and happy. Written in simple words, vividly illustrated with realistic scenes that relate to children's everyday lives, *You Are Healthy* is an ideal introduction to a lifetime of good health. *Paperback, full color, 8" x 8", 24 pages. Ages 4 & up.* MG117 **$8.99**

ISBN 978-1-934277-22-5

ISBN 978-1-934277-23-2

You Are Helpful *By Todd Snow, illustrated by Melodee Strong.* Children want to be helpful and are eager to become more independent. We see this whenever children insist "I can do it myself!" or "Let me!" This warm, inviting book introduces young children to age-appropriate ways to help out: put their toys away, get dressed by themselves, wait their turn, sit still at the doctor's office. Written in simple words, vividly illustrated with realistic scenes that relate to children's everyday lives, *You Are Helpful* lets children know they are competent and capable. *Paperback, full color, 8" x 8", 24 pages. Ages 4 & up.* MG118 **$8.99**

w w w . m a r e n g r e e n . c o m

5525 Memorial Avenue North, Suite 6 • Oak Park Heights, MN 55082
phone 800-287-1512 • 651-439-4500 • fax 651-439-4532 • email orders@marengreen.com